MathSmart

Math Games

Grade 2

Printed in China

CONTENTS Math Games • Grade Two

1 Homeward-Bound

Count by 1's from 125 to 160 and colour the path. Help Billy the Horse find the way home.

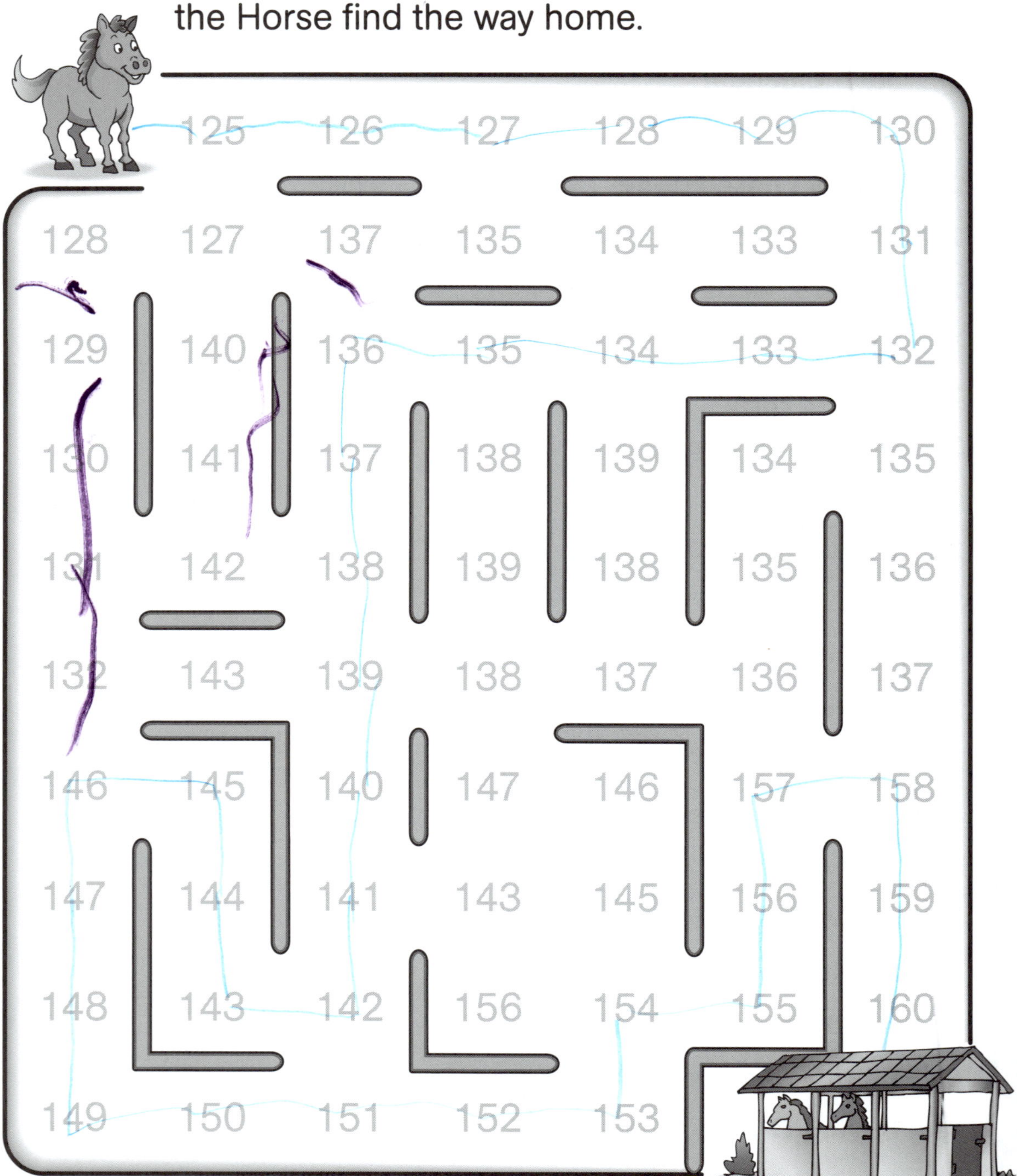

2 Two Pretty Girls

Mary and Susan are looking into the mirrors. Help them complete their mirror images.

3 A Torn Calendar

Joe has torn the calendar by mistake. Help him colour the torn piece that matches the calendar below. Then answer the questions.

Oct

S	M	T
		1
6	7	8
13	14	15
20	21	22
27	28	29

①

Ⓐ **ober**

W	T	F	S
2	3	4	5
9	10	11	12
16	17	18	19
23	24	25	26
30			

Ⓑ **ober**

W	T	F	S
2	3	4	5
9	10	11	12
16	17	18	19
23	24	25	26

Ⓒ **ober**

W	T	F	S
2	3	4	5
9	10	11	12
16	17	18	19
23	24	25	26
30	31		

② How many Mondays are there? ______________

③ What are the dates? ______________

④ How many Thursdays are there? ______________

⑤ What are the dates? ______________

4 Good Helpers

Find out how long each child takes to do the jobs. Then answer the questions.

Daisy

Sam

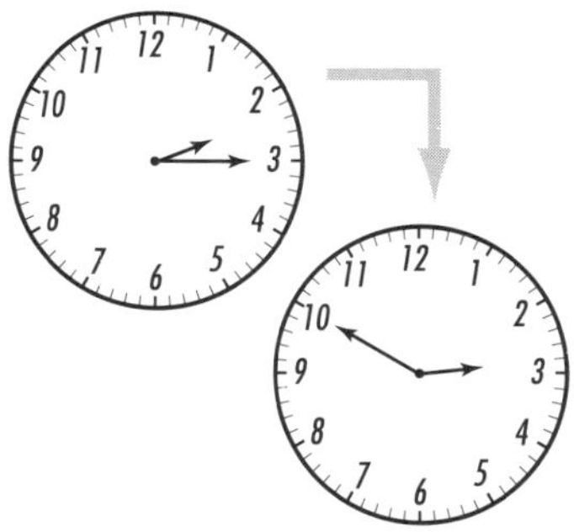

① ______ min

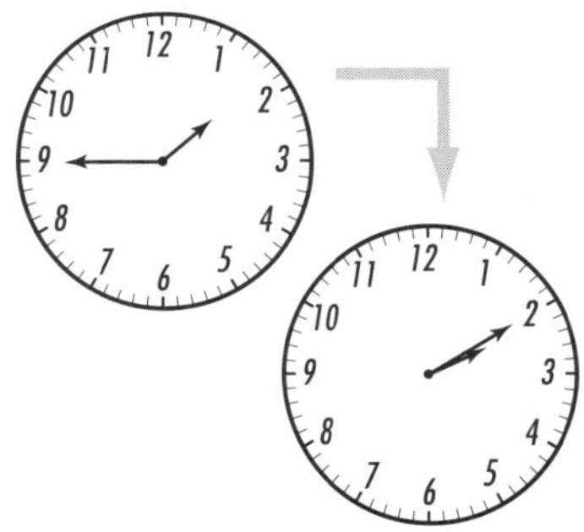

② ______ min

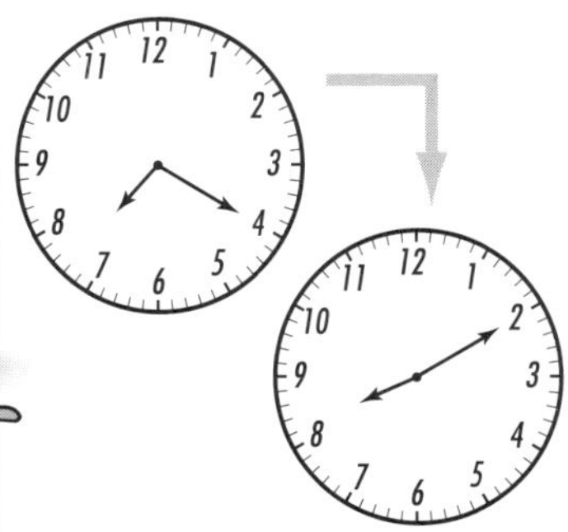

③ ______ min

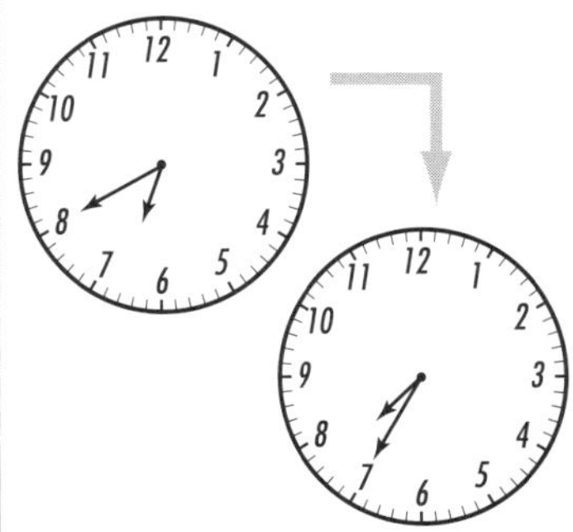

④ ______ min

⑤ Who takes less time to wash a car? __________

⑥ Who takes less time to make a cake? __________

5 Joe's Favourite CDs

Look at Joe's CD collection. Help him put the CDs in order from the one with the greatest code to the one with the least. Write the representing letters.

A

B

C

D

① In order: _____ , _____ , _____ , _____

I

J

K

L

② In order: _____ , _____ , _____ , _____

P

Q

R

S

③ In order: _____ , _____ , _____ , _____

6 Roger's Candies

Roger has a lot of candies. He puts every 5 candies into a bag. Circle every 5 candies to form a group. Then fill in the blanks.

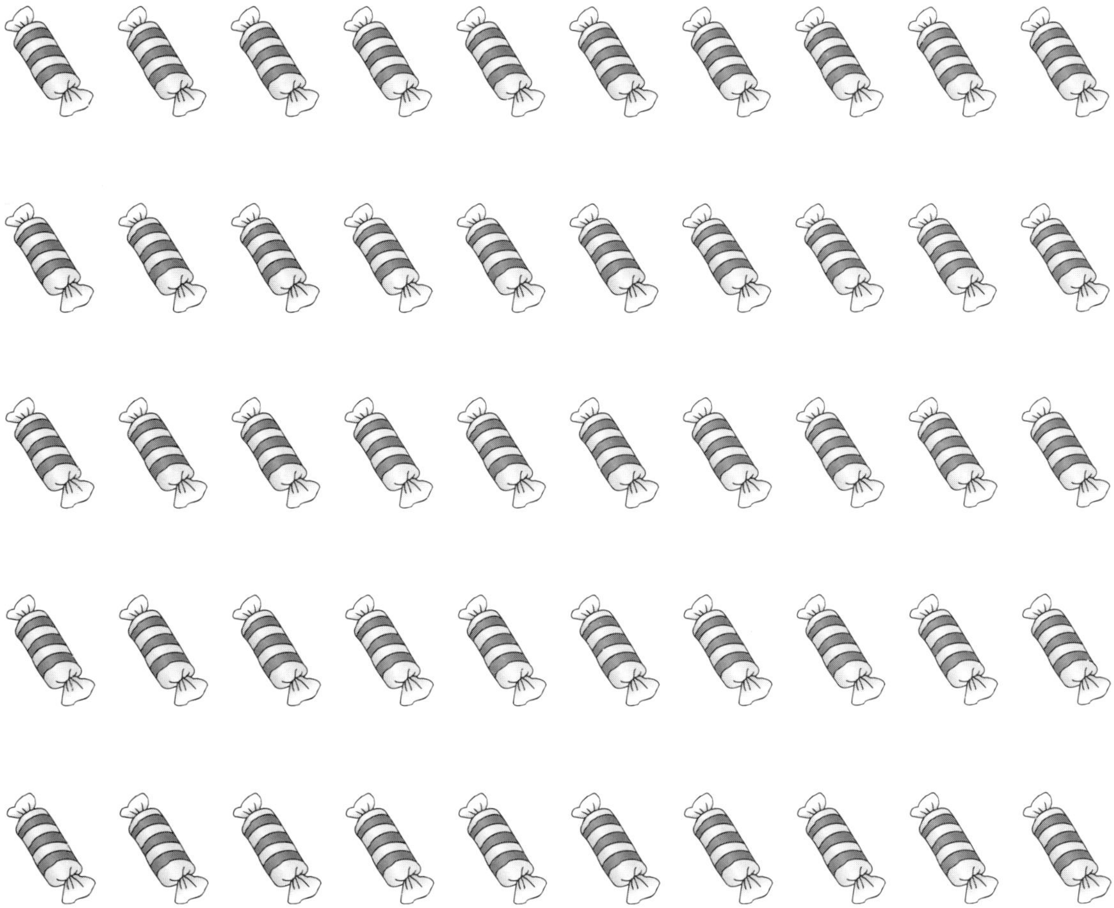

I have _____ candies. If I put every 5 candies into a bag, I need _____ bags in all.

7 Who's the Winner?

Read what the children say. Write their names in the blanks to show the order they finished the race.

Order: ______________ , ______________ , ______________ , ______________

1st 2nd 3rd 4th

The Heaviest Toy

Tommy is weighing his toys with some blocks. Help him complete the table and circle the heaviest toy.

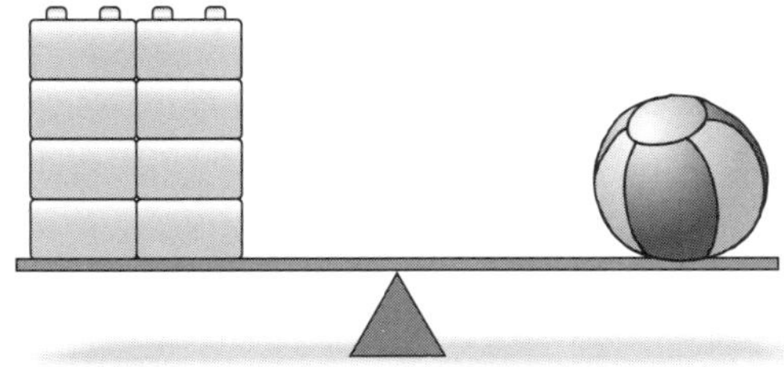

① as heavy as				

② The heaviest toy is  .

9 Making Cookies

Ted is cutting his cookies. Circle the cookies that are divided equally into quarters.

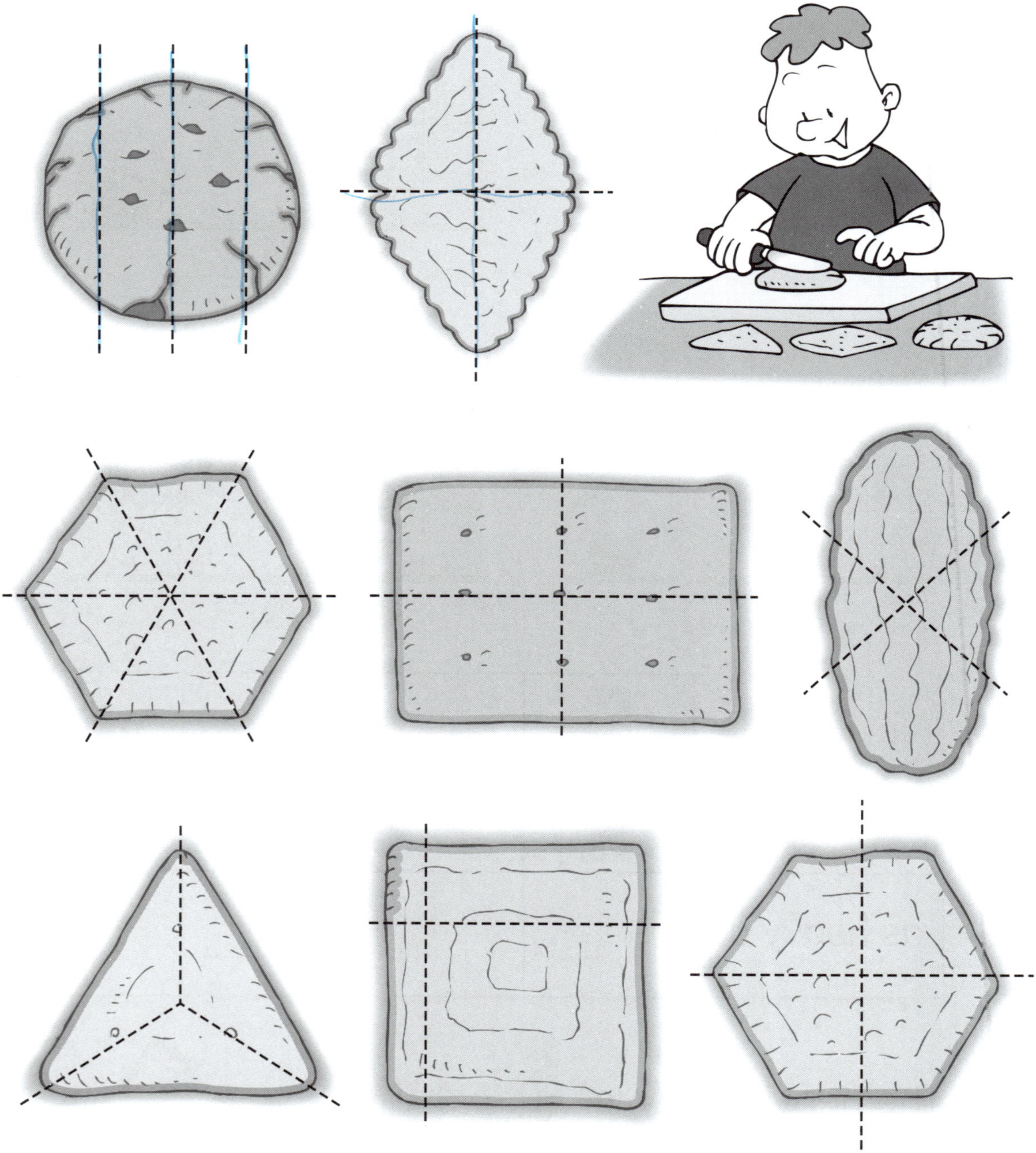

10 Who's the Honour Student?

Read what the teacher says. Colour the honour student.

The honour student does not have long hair. He / She does not wear glasses. He / She is beside one of the students with glasses. One of the students above him / her wears glasses, too. He / She is to the right of one of the girls.

11 Pizza Day

See how the children cut their pizzas on Pizza Day. Help them write the fraction for the shaded part of each pizza.

①

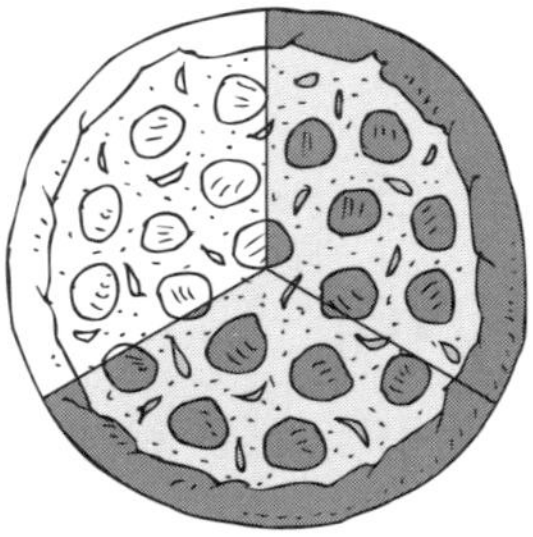

______

②

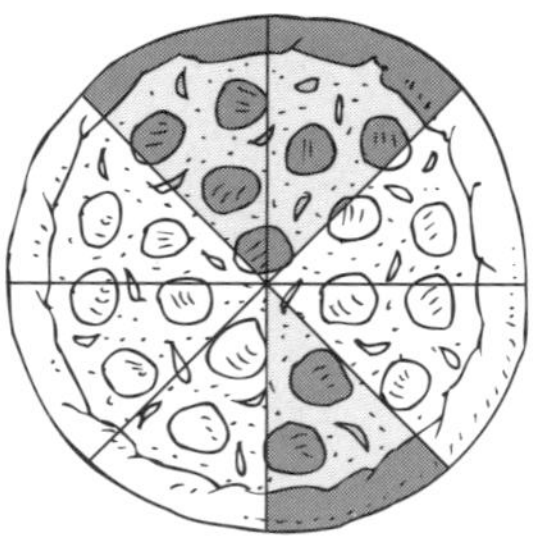

______

③

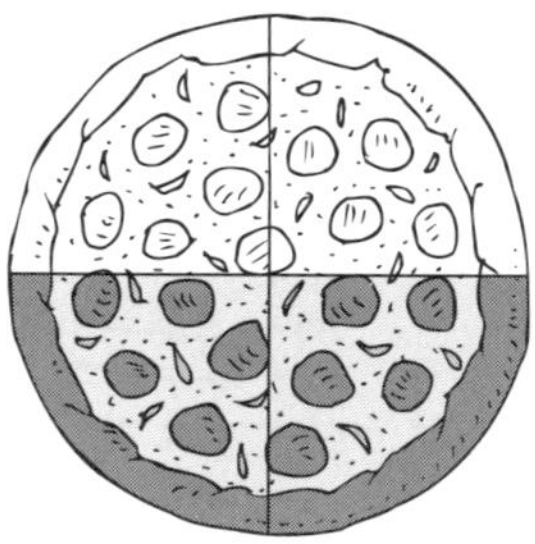

______

④

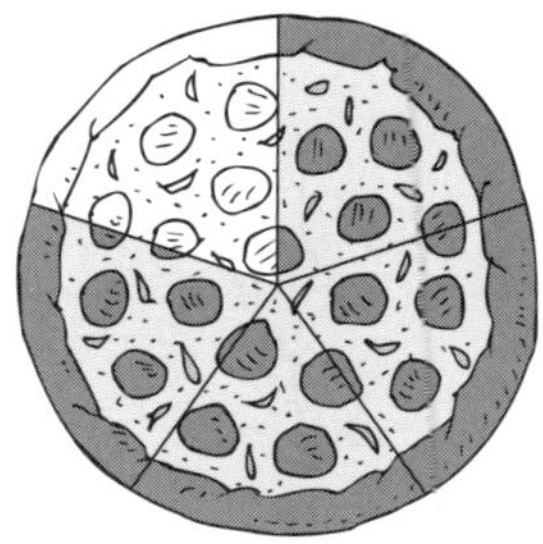

______

⑤

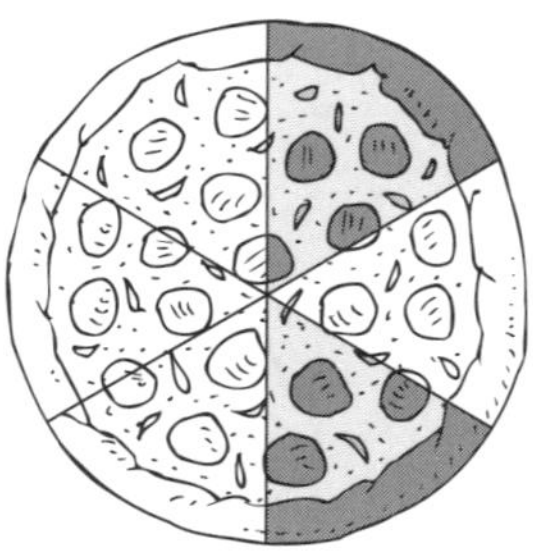

______

⑥

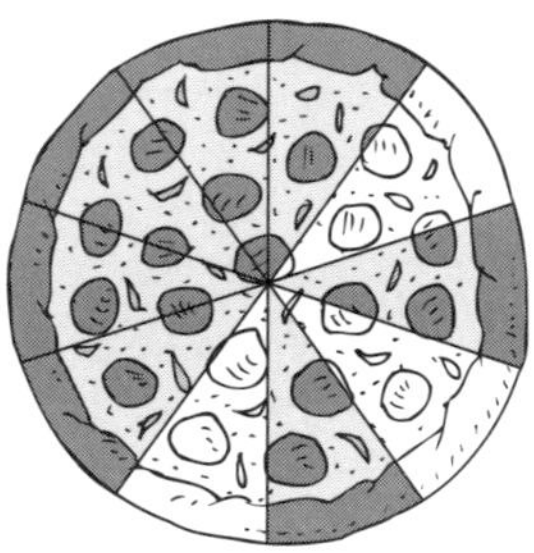

______

⑦

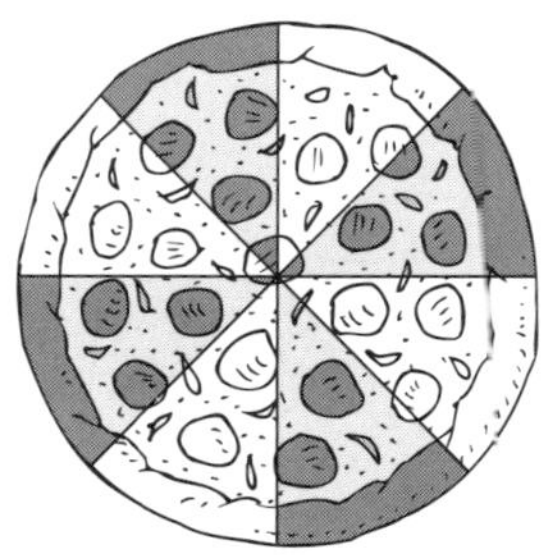

______

12 At the Souvenir Shop

Mrs. Venn is buying 1 souvenir for each student in her class. Read what she says, complete the graph and answer the questions.

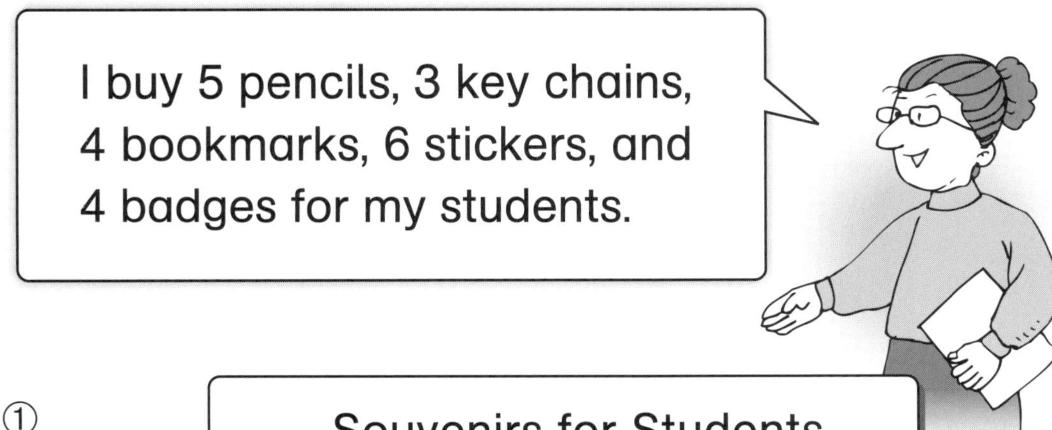

① Souvenirs for Students

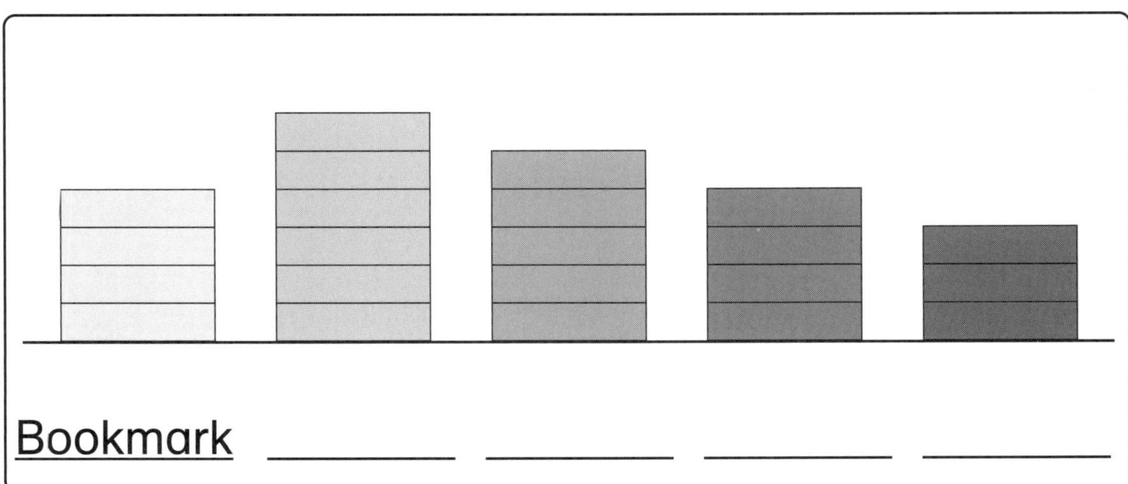

② How many students are in Mrs. Venn's class? ________

③ If each badge costs $2, how much does Mrs. Venn need to pay for the badges? ________

13 Jessica's Toys on the Shelves

Jessica has put all her toys on the shelves. Look at her toys. Help Jessica circle the correct words or picture.

① The  is to the **left / right** of the  .

② The  is to the **left / right** of the  .

③ The  is **above / below** the  .

④ The  is **above / below** the  .

⑤ The 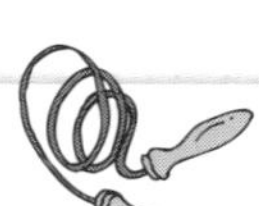 /  is beside the  .

14 Tim's Building Blocks

Help Tim write the numbers on the building blocks. Then complete what he says.

①

②

③
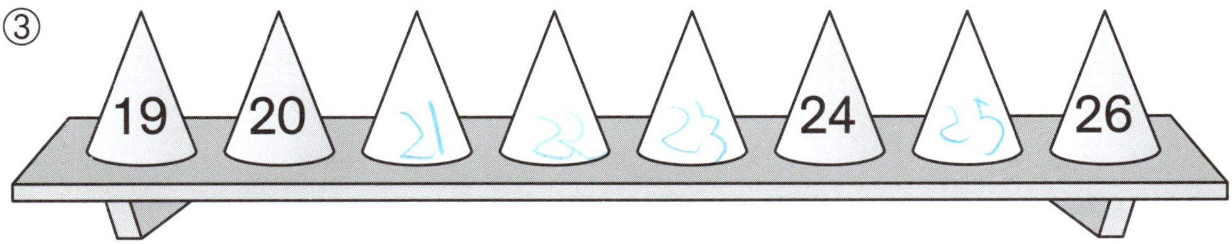

④
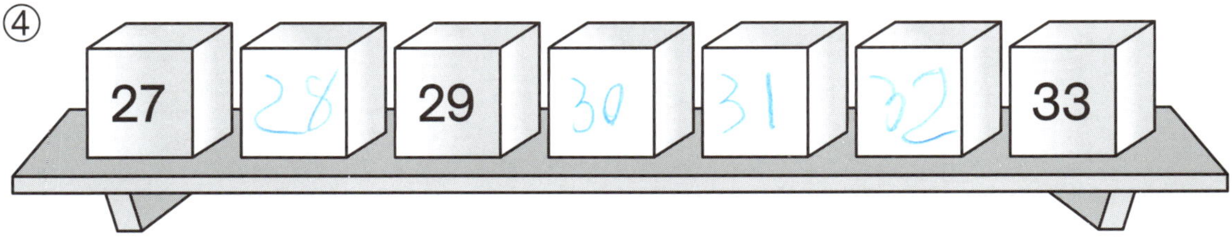

⑤

I have ________ building blocks in all.

There are ________ prisms, ________ cubes,

________ cylinders, and ________ cones.

15 What's for Lunch?

The children spin the following spinners to see what they have for lunch. Help them colour the correct pictures to complete the sentences.

①

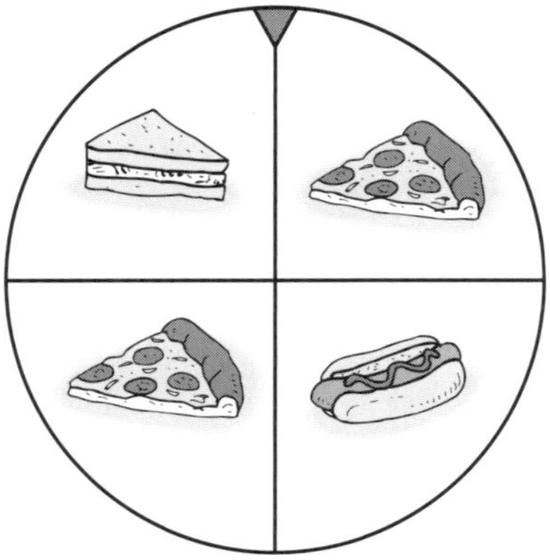

It is impossible to get a

 .

It is more likely to get a

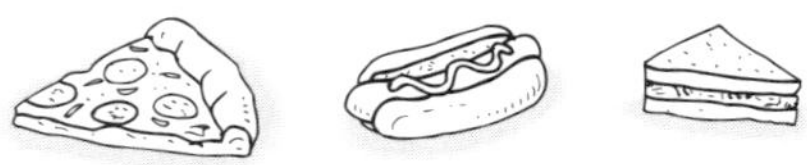 .

②

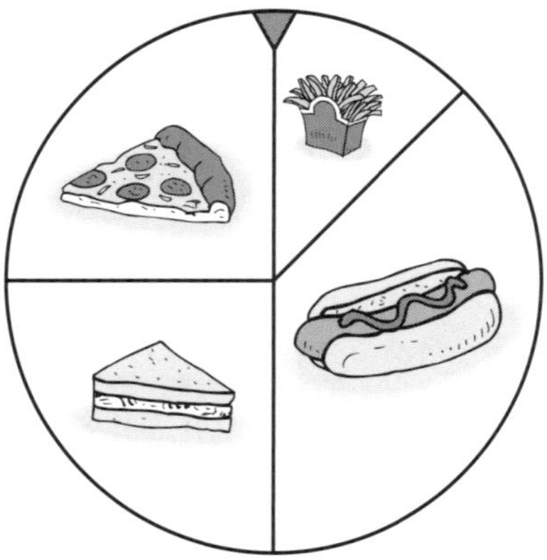

It is less likely to get a

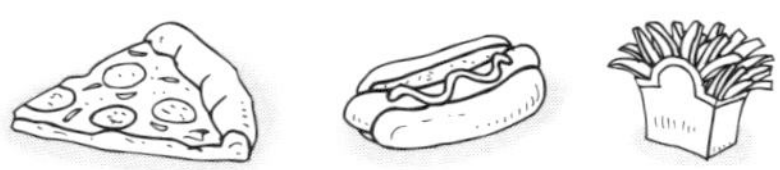 .

It has an equal chance to get a

 and a  .

③

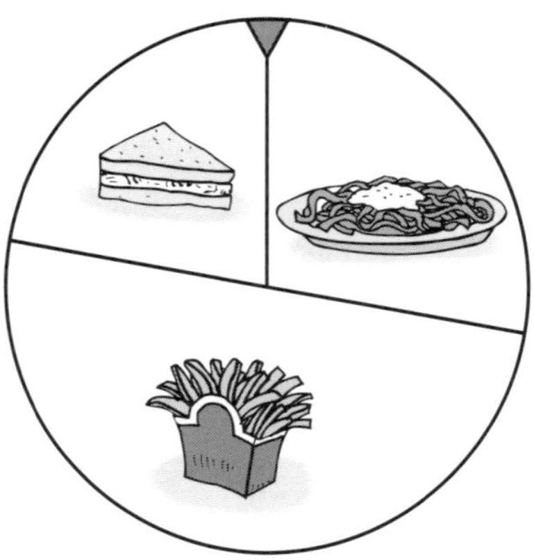

It is impossible to get a

 .

It is less likely to get a

 .

16 Angela's Candies

Angela is putting her candies into jars. Help her find the number of candies in some of the bags.

①
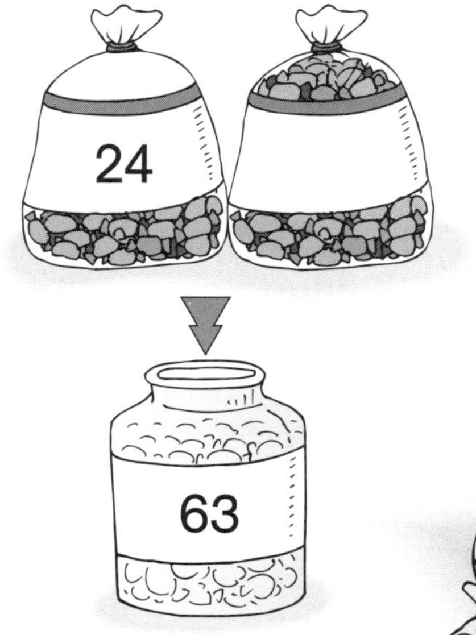

②
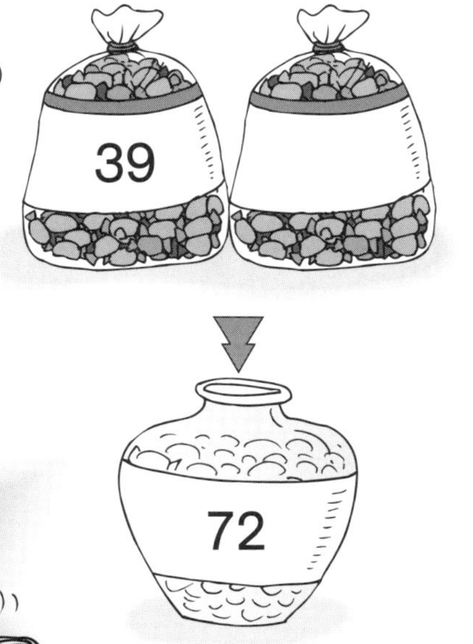

③
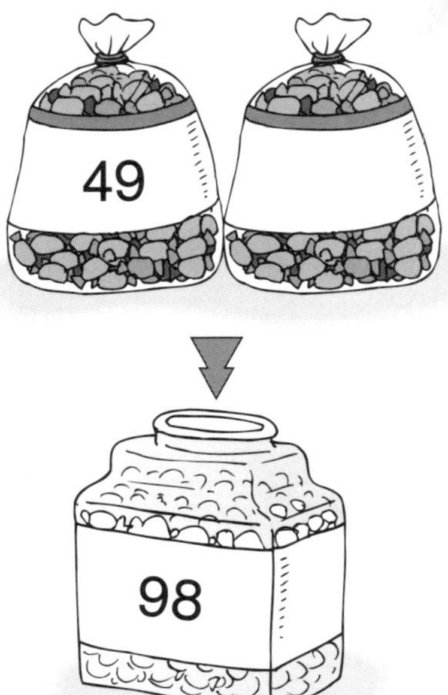

④
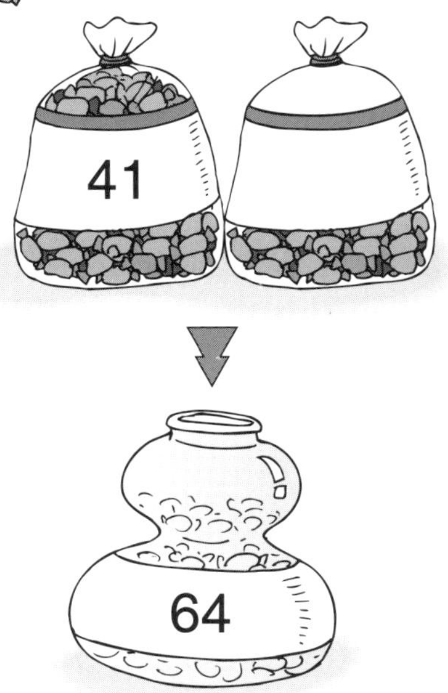

17 At the Fruit Market

The Welch family are at the fruit market. Help them solve the problems.

① 3 baskets of apples

3 groups of 4 = 3 x 4 = ____

② 4 bunches of bananas

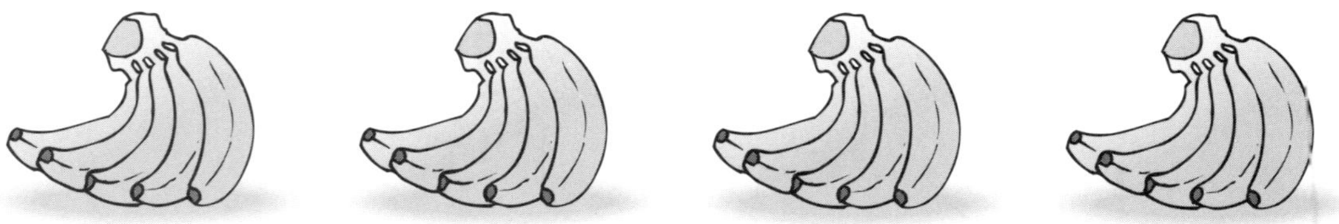

4 groups of 5 = 4 x ____ = ____

③ 6 bags of corn

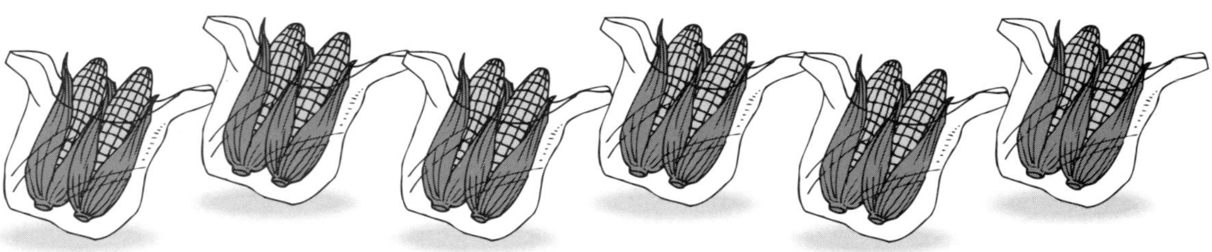

6 groups of 2 = 6 x ____ = ____

④ 5 baskets of celery

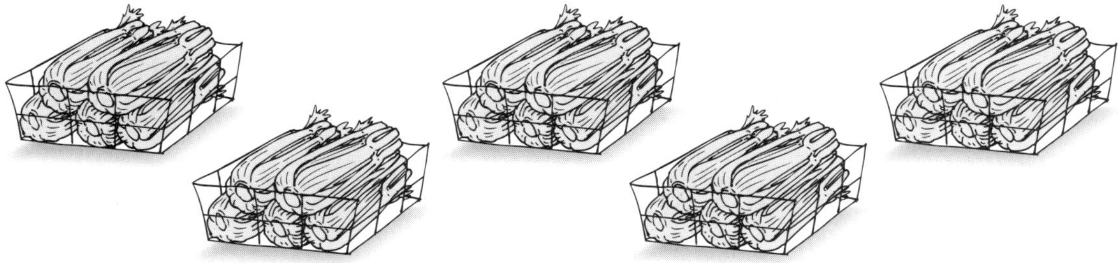

5 groups of 5 = 5 x _____ = _____

⑤ 3 bags of carrots

3 groups of 8 = 3 x _____ = _____

⑥ 6 boxes of onions

6 groups of 9 = 6 x _____ = _____

18 Drawing Shapes

Read the rules and connect the dots to complete the shapes.

1st shape : Count backward from 20 to 17 by 1's.

2nd shape : Count forward from 22 to 26 by 2's.

3rd shape : Count forward from 20 to 45 by 5's.

4th shape : Count forward from 10 to 40 by 10's.

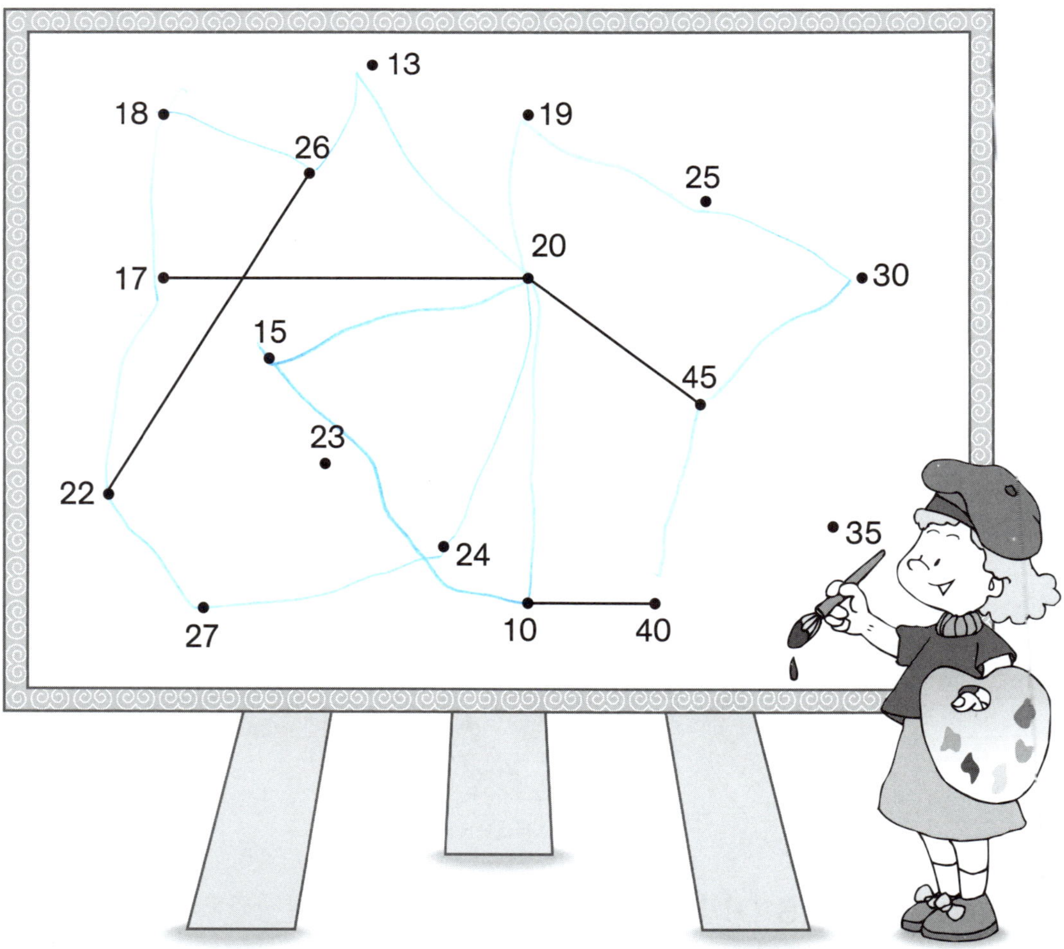

19 An Alien Race

Colour the runners.

Colour the 2nd, 8th, 11th, and 16th runners blue.

Colour the 3rd, 9th, 14th, and 19th runners yellow.

Colour the 5th, 10th, 15th, and 22nd runners green.

20 Quarter-Turned Pictures

The children each make two $\frac{1}{4}$ turns of their picture. Help them draw the pictures.

①

②

③

21 Measuring Devices

Choose the most appropriate thing to measure the length of each of the following objects. Draw the lines.

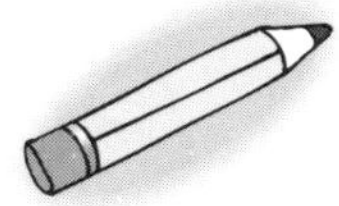

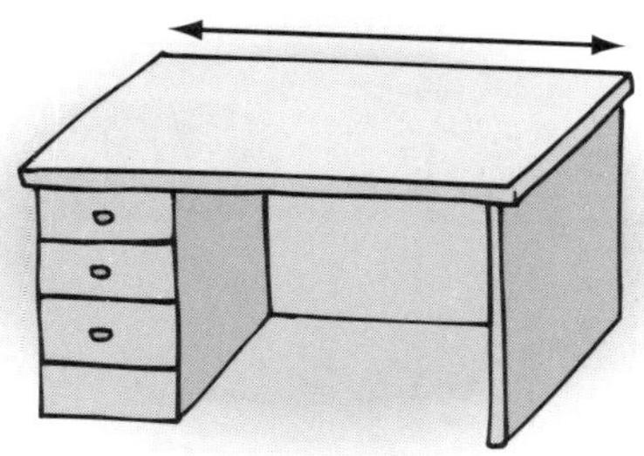

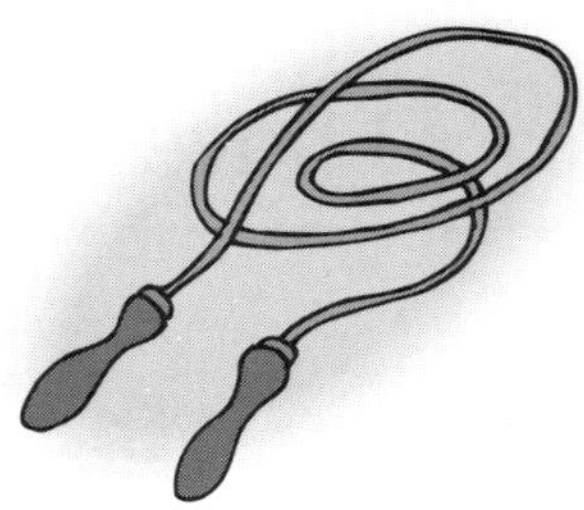

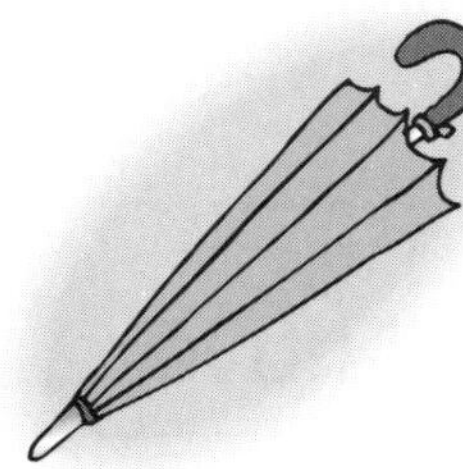

22 Who Has the Most?

Count the number of tokens each child has by 2's or 5's. Write the numbers in words to complete what the children say. Find out who has the most tokens.

① I have ____________________ tokens.

Mary

② I have ____________________ tokens.

Nathan

③ I have ____________________ tokens.

Betsy

ANSWERS

1 Homeward-Bound

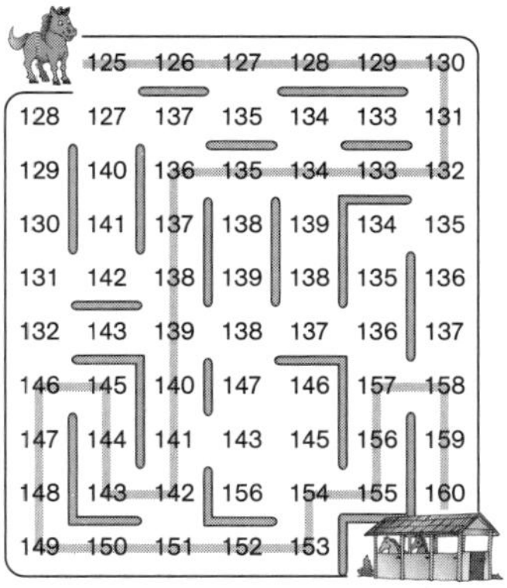

2 Two Pretty Girls

3 A Torn Calendar

1. C
2. 4
3. 7th, 14th, 21st, 28th
4. 5
5. 3rd, 10th, 17th, 24th, 31st

4 Good Helpers

1. 35
2. 25
3. 50
4. 55
5. Sam
6. Daisy

5 Joe's Favourite CDs

1. B ; C ; A ; D
2. K ; J ; L ; I
3. P ; S ; R ; Q

6 Roger's Candies

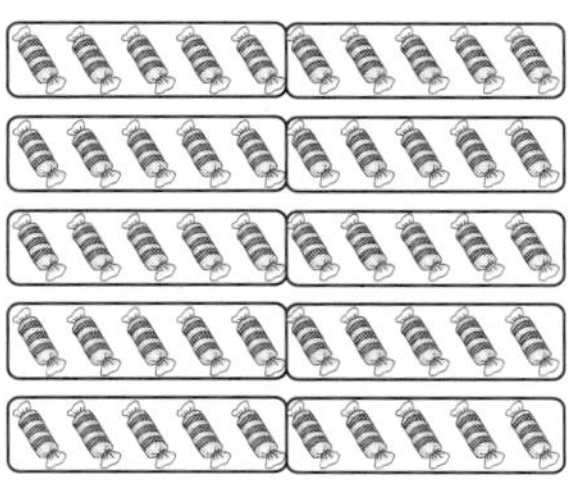

50 ; 10

7 Who's the Winner?

Peter ; Anna ; Mabel ; Jack

8 The Heaviest Toy

1. 12 ; 8 ; 5 ; 7
2. 

9 Making Cookies

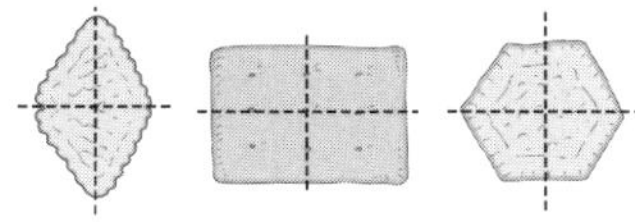

10 Who's the Honour Student?

11 Pizza Day

1. $\frac{2}{3}$
2. $\frac{3}{8}$
3. $\frac{2}{4}$
4. $\frac{4}{5}$
5. $\frac{2}{6}$
6. $\frac{7}{10}$
7. $\frac{4}{8}$

12 At the Souvenir Shop

1. Sticker ; Pencil ; Badge ; Key chain
2. 22
3. $8

13 Jessica's Toys on the Shelves

1. right
2. left
3. below
4. above
5. 

14 Tim's Building Blocks

1. 3 ; 4 ; 6 ; 7
2. 10 ; 12 ; 13 ; 14 ; 17
3. 21 ; 22 ; 23 ; 25
4. 28 ; 30 ; 31 ; 32
5. 33 ; 8 ; 7 ; 10 ; 8

ANSWERS

15 What's for Lunch?

1. 
2. 
3. 

16 Angela's Candies

1. 39
2. 33
3. 49
4. 23

17 At the Fruit Market

1. 12
2. 5 ; 20
3. 2 ; 12
4. 5 ; 25
5. 8 ; 24
6. 9 ; 54

18 Drawing Shapes

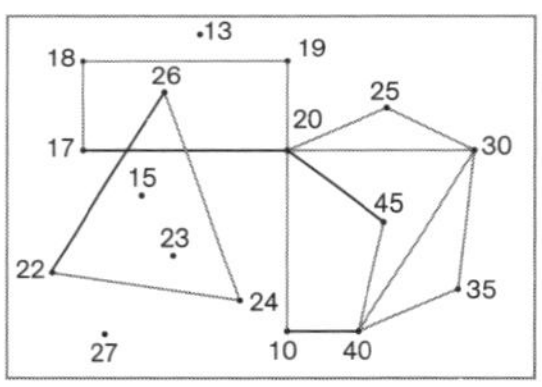

19 An Alien Race

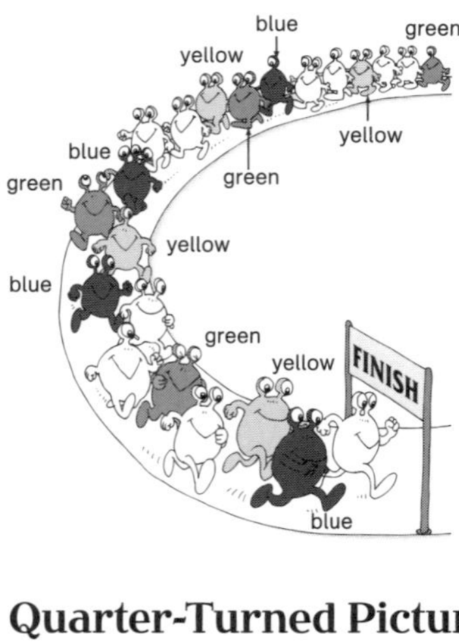

20 Quarter-Turned Pictures

1. 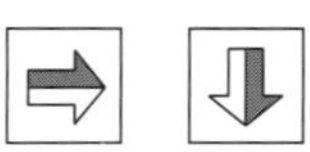
2. 
3. 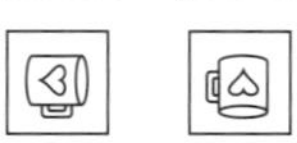

21 Measuring Devices

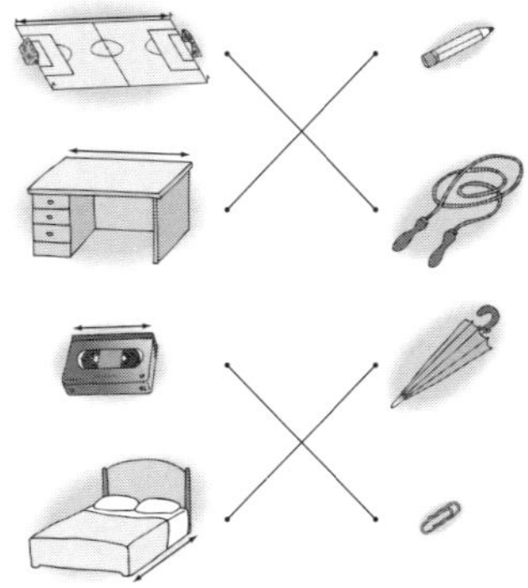

22 Who Has the Most?

1. sixteen
2. fifteen
3. eighteen
4. fourteen
5. ten
6. twelve
7. Betsy

23 Emma's Stickers

1. 7
2. 5
3. 5
4. 2
5. 3

24 Generous David

1. 2
2. 4
3. 3

25 Jill's Calendar

1. June
2. May
3. September
4. August
5. July

26 Drying the Towels

27 Sally's Photo Frame

28 In the Gift Shop

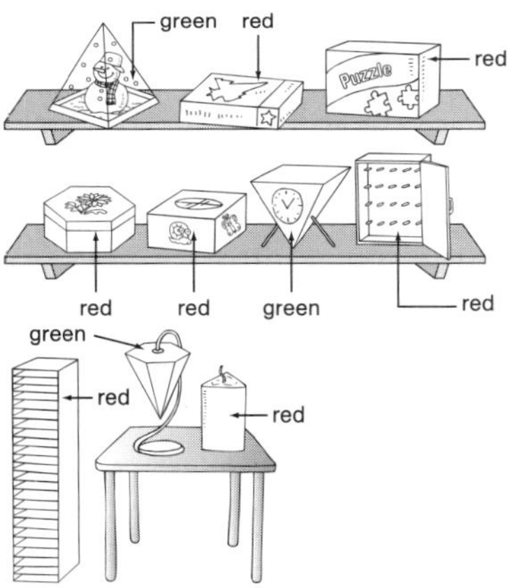

29 Spiders' Webs

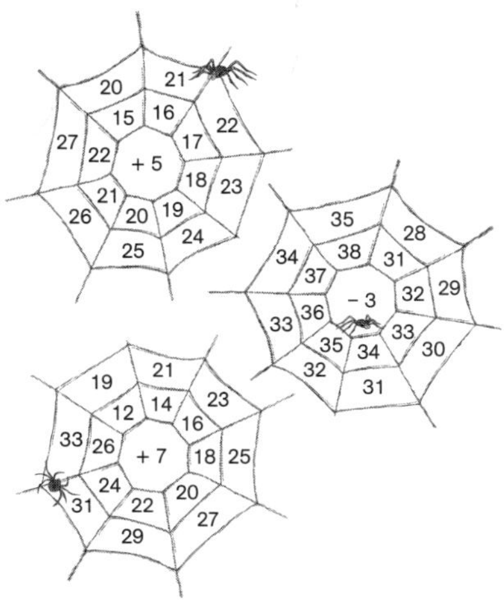

30 Christmas Cards

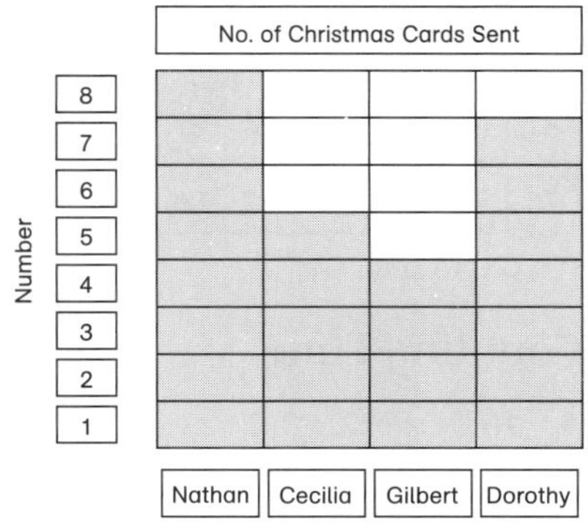

31 Fruit Display

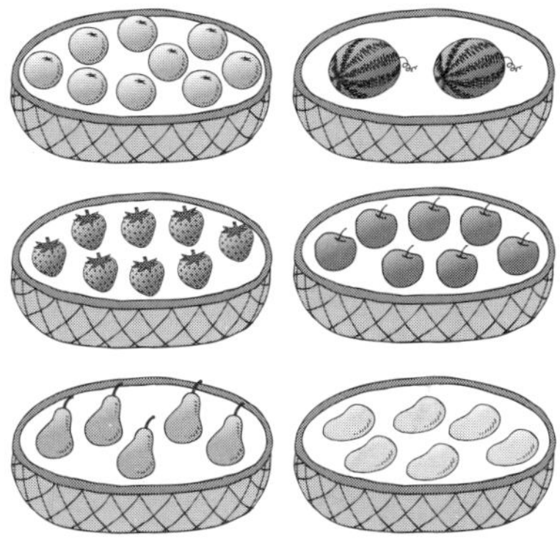

32 Household Chores

33 Card Games

1. Yes 2. No 3. No
4. No 5. No 6. Yes

34 What's Robin Doing?

1. slide 2. turn
3. flip 4. turn

35 Lost in the Park

b 18	a 68	p 83	w 38	m 82	t 8	l 58	i 86
a 81	m 60	s 78	c 80	d 34	t 87	e 62	p 48
k 75	e 89	n 36	c 99	y 28	s 85	f 98	s 42

c a m p s i t e

36 Counting Time

1. 15
2. 8
3. 50
4. 12
5. 20

37 Jason's Crayons

1. 8 ; 8
2. 8 ; 16
3. 8 ; 24
4. 8 ; 32
5. 8 ; 40
6. 8 ; 48
7. 8 ; 56
8. 8 ; 64
9. 8 ; 72
10. 8 ; 80

38 Buying Toys

1. 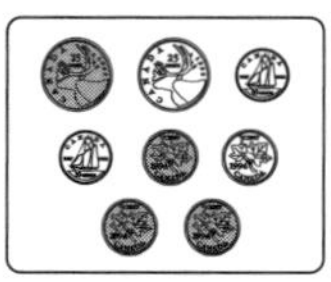
2. 
3. 
4. 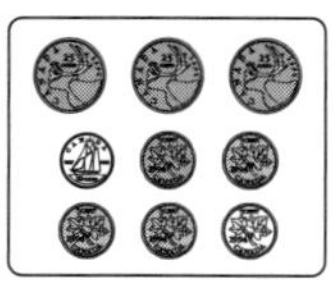

39 Yummy Ice Cream Cones

1. Number of Ice Cream Cones Sold
2. Caramel
3. 20

40 Picnic Time

1. $\frac{7}{10}$
2. $\frac{6}{12}$
3. $\frac{2}{8}$
4. $\frac{4}{6}$

41 Freddie's Apples

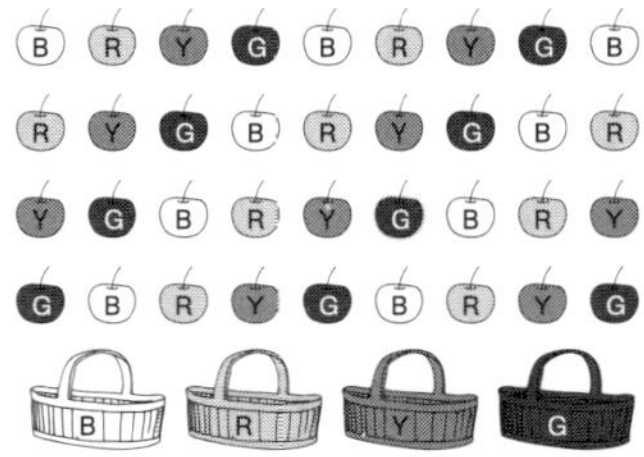

9

42 Measuring Temperatures

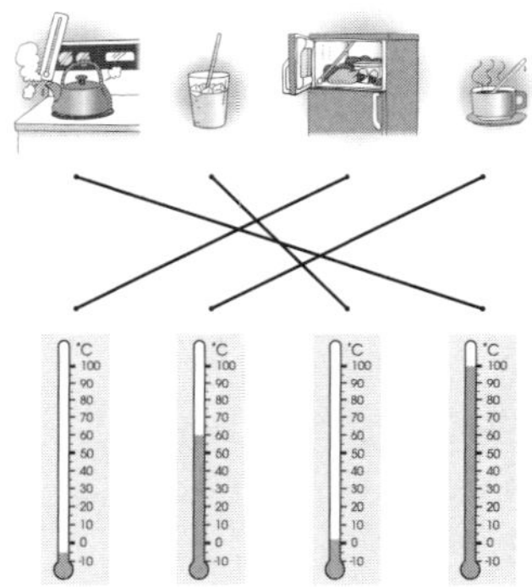

43 Good Business

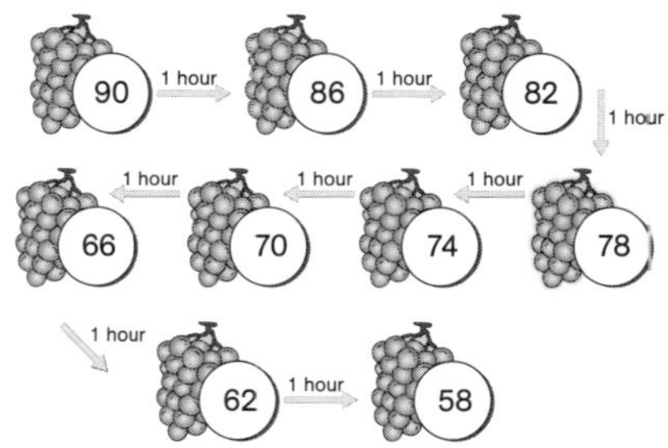

58

44 Edith's Shapes

1. $\frac{3}{12}$
2. $\frac{3}{12}$
3. $\frac{2}{12}$
4. $\frac{2}{12}$
5. $\frac{6}{12}$

45 Buying Drinks

1. 64
2. 7
3. 37
4. 94

④ I have ____________________ tokens.

Rebecca

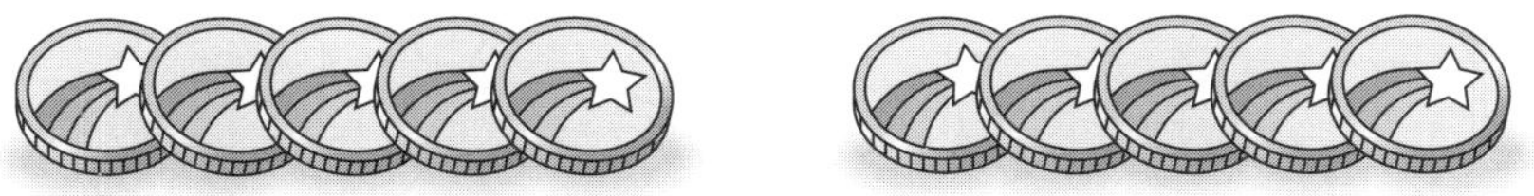

⑤ I have ____________________ tokens.

Colin

⑥ I have ____________________ tokens.

Doris

⑦ ____________________ has the most tokens.

23 Emma's Stickers

Look at Emma's stickers. Fill in the correct numbers to complete what Emma says.

① _____ out of 12 stickers are animals.

② _____ out of 12 stickers are plants.

③ _____ out of 12 stickers are animals with glasses.

④ _____ out of 12 stickers are trees.

⑤ _____ out of 12 stickers are dogs with a cap.

24 Generous David

David is sharing his treats with his friends. Help him find how many treats each child can get.

① Each child gets _____  .

② Each child gets _____  .

③ Each child gets _____  .

25 Jill's Calendar

Jill has made a calendar from April to September. Help her name the months in her calendar.

April

Sun	Mon	Tue	Wed	Thu	Fri	Sat
	1	2	3	4	5	6
7	8	9	10	11	12	13
14	15	16	17	18	19	20
21	22	23	24	25	26	27
28	29	30				

①

Sun	Mon	Tue	Wed	Thu	Fri	Sat
						1
2	3	4	5	6	7	8
9	10	11	12	13	14	15
16	17	18	19	20	21	22
23	24	25	26	27	28	29
30						

②

Sun	Mon	Tue	Wed	Thu	Fri	Sat
			1	2	3	4
5	6	7	8	9	10	11
12	13	14	15	16	17	18
19	20	21	22	23	24	25
26	27	28	29	30	31	

③

Sun	Mon	Tue	Wed	Thu	Fri	Sat
1	2	3	4	5	6	7
8	9	10	11	12	13	14
15	16	17	18	19	20	21
22	23	24	25	26	27	28
29	30					

④

Sun	Mon	Tue	Wed	Thu	Fri	Sat
				1	2	3
4	5	6	7	8	9	10
11	12	13	14	15	16	17
18	19	20	21	22	23	24
25	26	27	28	29	30	31

⑤

Sun	Mon	Tue	Wed	Thu	Fri	Sat
	1	2	3	4	5	6
7	8	9	10	11	12	13
14	15	16	17	18	19	20
21	22	23	24	25	26	27
28	29	30	31			

26 Drying the Towels

Add or subtract. Help the children find their own towels. Pair up the baskets and the towels with the same answers. Colour them the same colour.

27 Sally's Photo Frame

Connect the dots with the same answers to see how Sally's photo frame looks like.

28 + 29

7 + 47

25 + 38

16 + 54

10 + 60

32 + 22

27 + 30

4 + 59

23 − 16

40 − 22

46 − 31

73 − 62

96 − 85

80 − 73

50 − 35

55 − 37

28 In the Gift Shop

Betty and Aunt Sue are in the gift shop. Look at the gifts and help them colour the pyramids green and the prisms red.

29 Spiders' Webs

Look at the spiders' webs. Complete the number patterns.

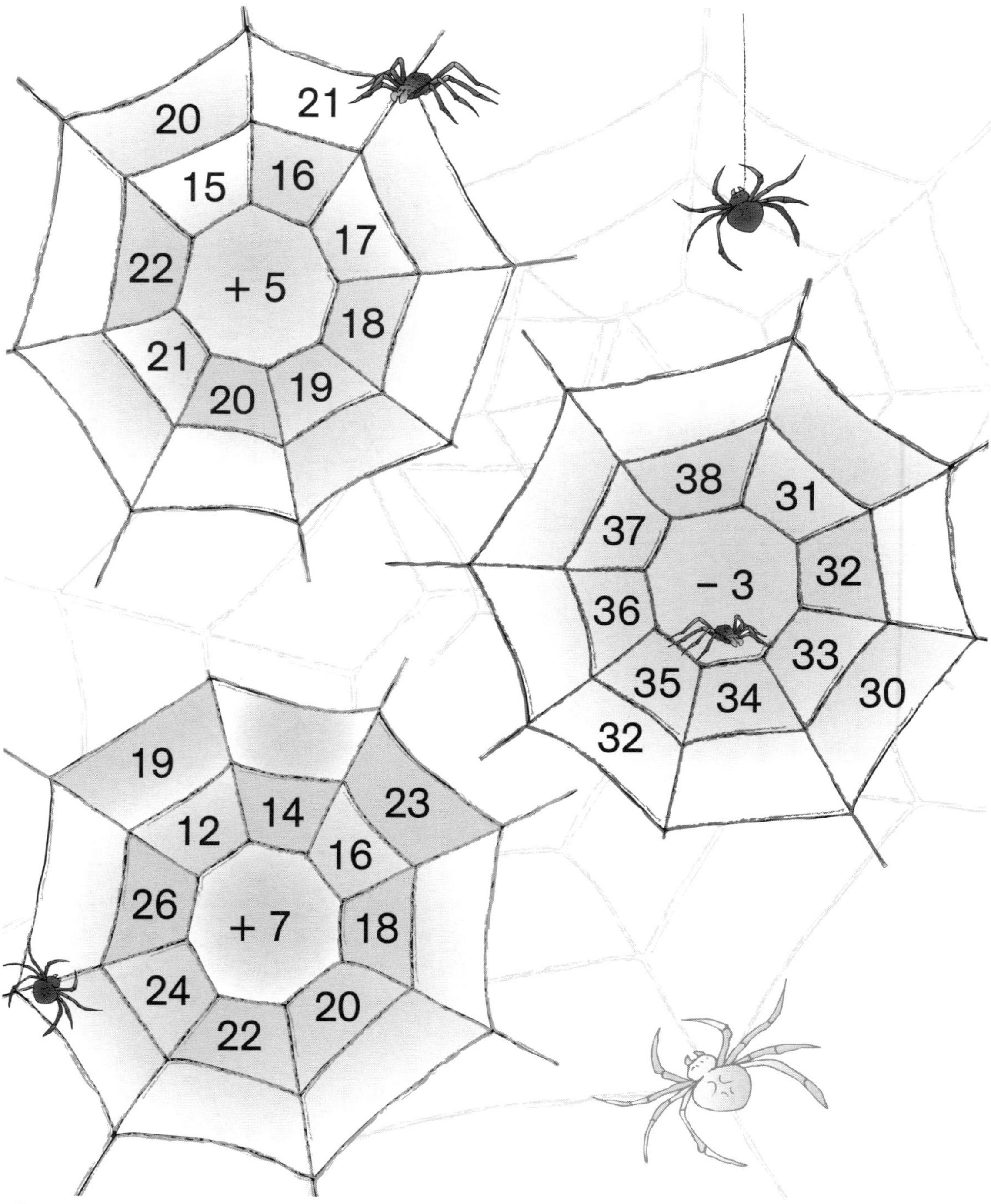

30 Christmas Cards

See how many Christmas cards each child sent last year.
Help them complete the graph to show the data.

	Nathan	Cecilia	Gilbert	Dorothy
No. of Christmas Cards Sent	8	5	4	7

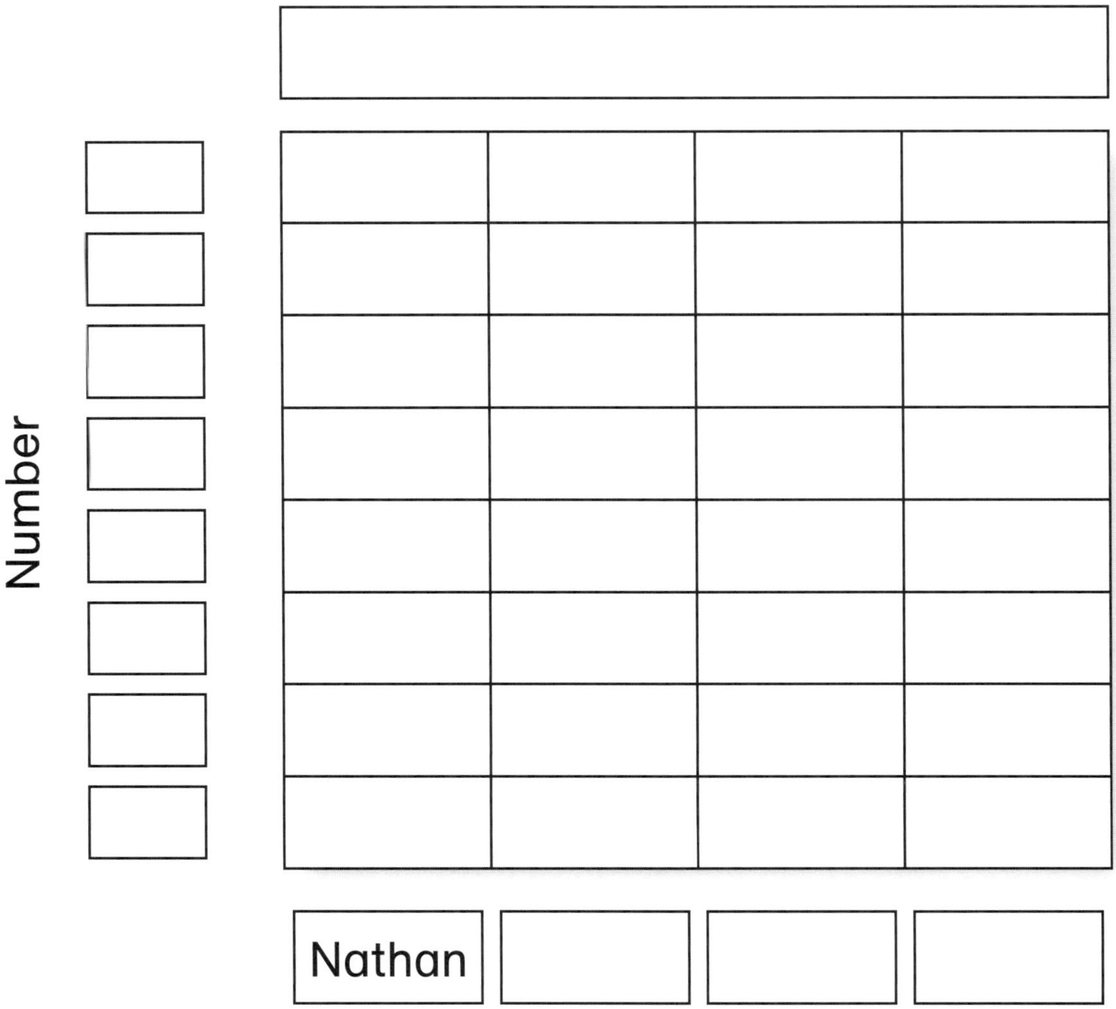

31 Fruit Display

Subtract. Draw the same number of each kind of fruit as the answer.

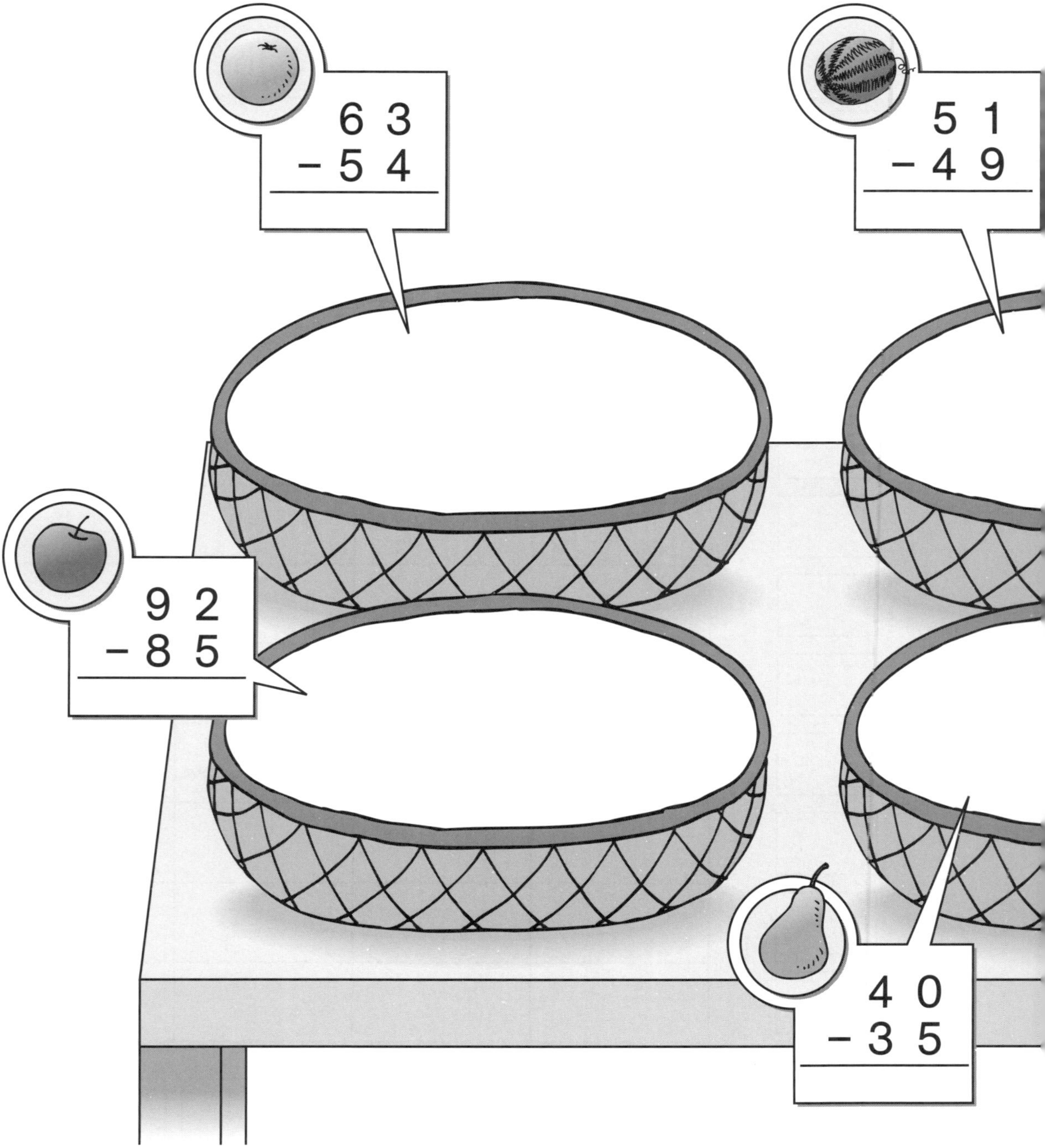

84
− 76
73
− 67

32 Household Chores

See how long the children took to finish their jobs. Help them draw the clock hands to show the finishing times.

①

②

③

33 Card Games

Ted shuffles his cards and lets his brother pick one from each group. Look at the cards in each group and help Ted's brother answer the questions.

① Is it likely to pick a  ? ________

② Is it more likely to pick a  than a  ? ________

③ Is it possible to pick a  ? ________

④ Is it most likely to pick a  ? ________

⑤ Is it more likely to pick a  than a  ? ________

⑥ Is it possible to pick a  ? ________

34 What's Robin Doing?

Robin is showing a box of puzzle to his friends. Write 'flip', 'turn', or 'slide' to tell how Robin transforms his box of puzzle.

① 

____

② 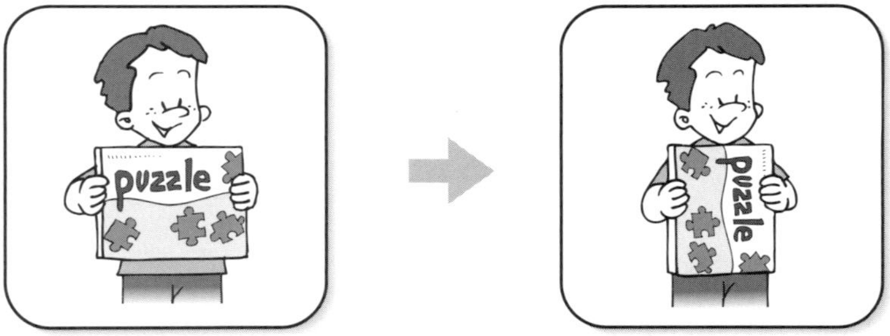

____

③ 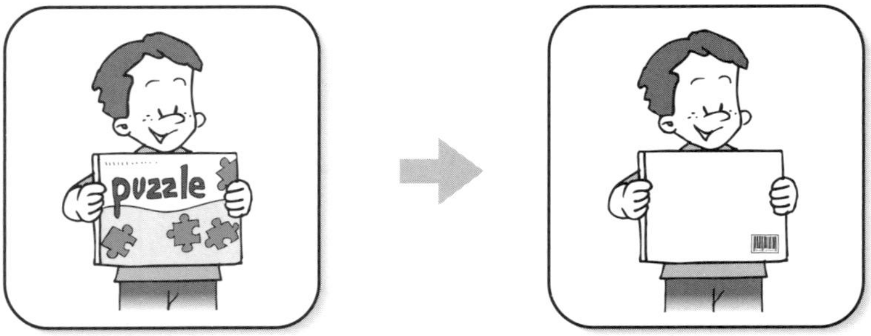

____

④ 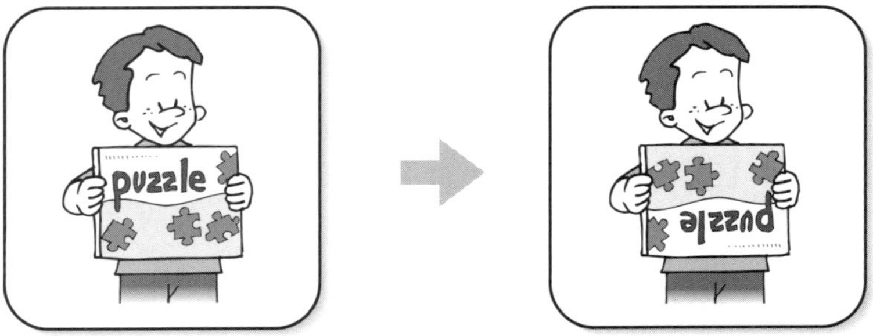

____

35 Lost in the Park

The children have lost their way in the park. Colour the numbers with 8 in the tens place. Put the coloured numbers in order from the smallest to the greatest. Write the representing letters in the blanks to complete what the guard says.

b 18	a 68	p 83	w 38	m 82	t 8	l 58	i 86
a 81	m 60	s 78	c 80	d 34	t 87	e 62	p 48
k 75	e 89	n 36	c 99	y 28	s 85	f 98	s 42

36 Counting Time

Read what the childen say. Help them count the things by 2's, 5's, or 10's. Then write the numbers.

①

Doris has _____  .

②

Nelson has _____  .

③

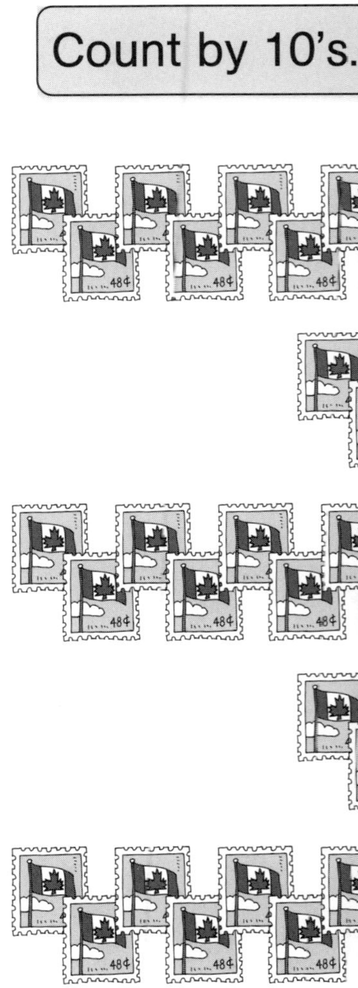

Kenneth h

_____  .

④

Toni has _____  .

⑤

Henry has _____  .

37 Jason's Crayons

Complete the multiplication sentences with the help of Jason's crayons.

① 1 group of 8 = 1 x _____ = _____

② 2 groups of 8 = 2 x _____ = _____

③ 3 groups of 8 = 3 x _____ = _____

④ 4 groups of 8 = 4 x _____ = _____

⑤ 5 groups of 8 = 5 x _____ = _____

⑥ 6 groups of 8 = 6 x _____ = _____

⑦ 7 groups of 8 = 7 x _____ = _____

⑧ 8 groups of 8 = 8 x _____ = _____

⑨ 9 groups of 8 = 9 x _____ = _____

⑩ 10 groups of 8 = 10 x _____ = _____

38 Buying Toys

Colour the coins Jason needs to pay for each toy.

①

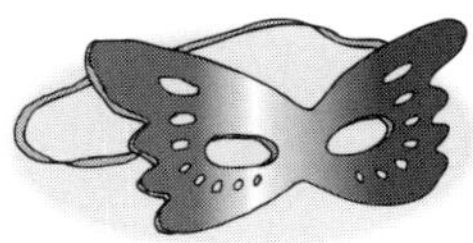

28¢

②

46¢

③

62¢

④

79¢

39 Yummy Ice Cream Cones

Look at the graph and answer the questions.

Number of Ice Cream Cones Sold

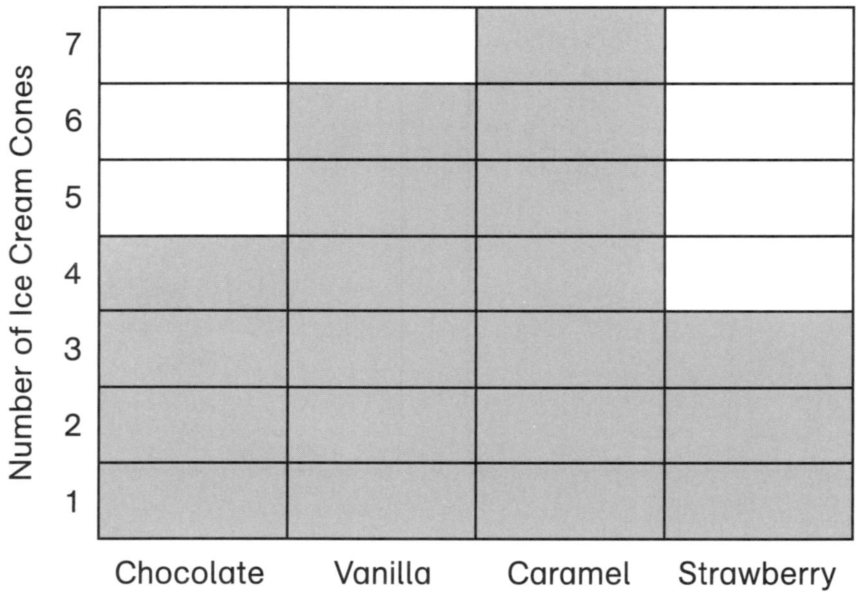

① What is the title of the graph?

____

② Which flavour of ice cream cones was sold the most?

____

③ How many ice cream cones were sold in all?

____

40 Picnic Time

Katie and her family had a picnic yesterday. See how much food was left. Write fractions to complete what they say.

①

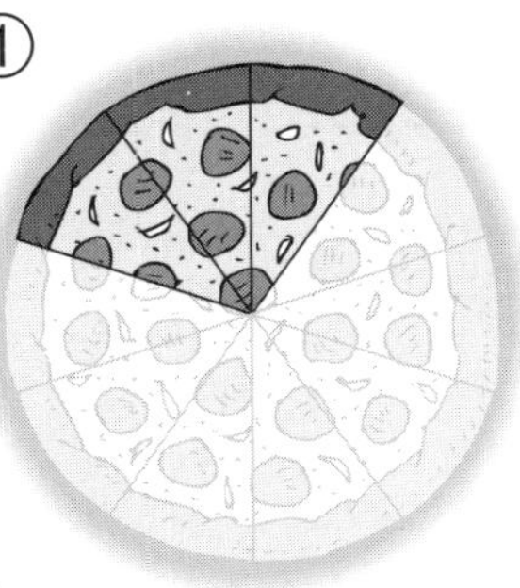

We ate _____ of a pizza.

②

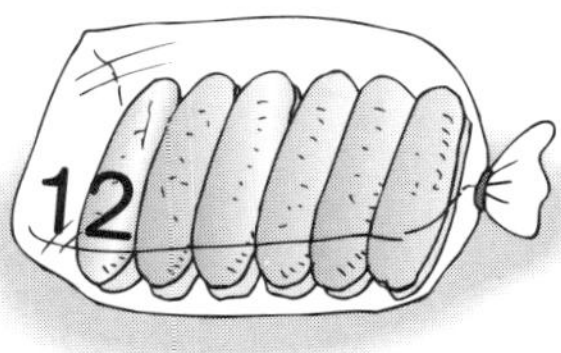

We ate _____ of a bag of buns.

③

We ate _____ of a packet of sausages.

④

We ate _____ of a box of muffins.

41 Freddie's Apples

Freddie divides 36 apples equally and puts them into 4 baskets. Help him colour the apples and the baskets to match the colours specified. Then count the apples with the same colour and complete what Freddie says.

B- Blue R- Red Y- Yellow G- Green

B	R	Y	G	B	R	Y	G	B
R	Y	G	B	R	Y	G	B	R
Y	G	B	R	Y	G	B	R	Y
G	B	R	Y	G	B	R	Y	G

There are ________ apples in each basket.

42 Measuring Temperatures

Joseph is measuring the temperatures of the following things. Draw lines to match the things with the correct thermometers.

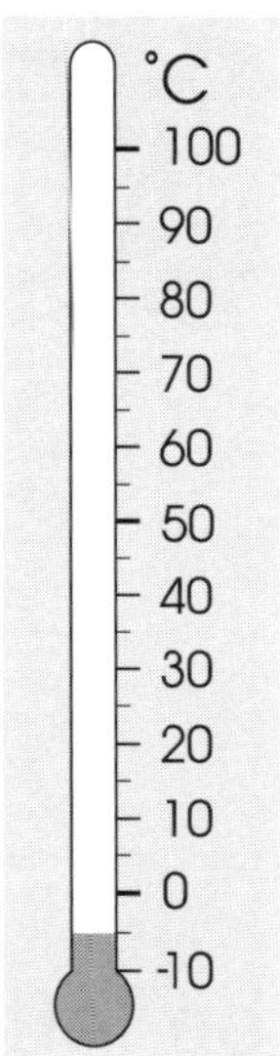

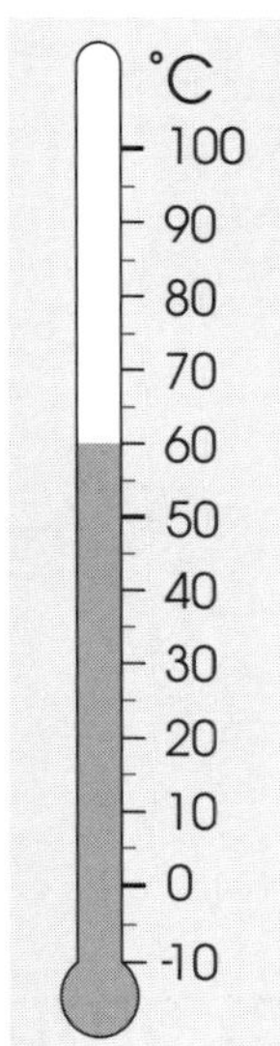

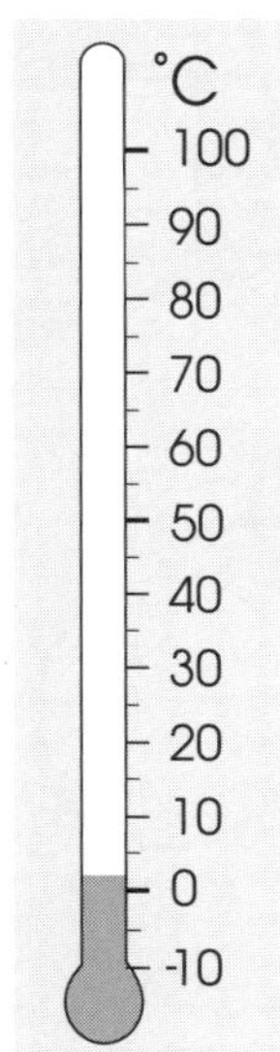

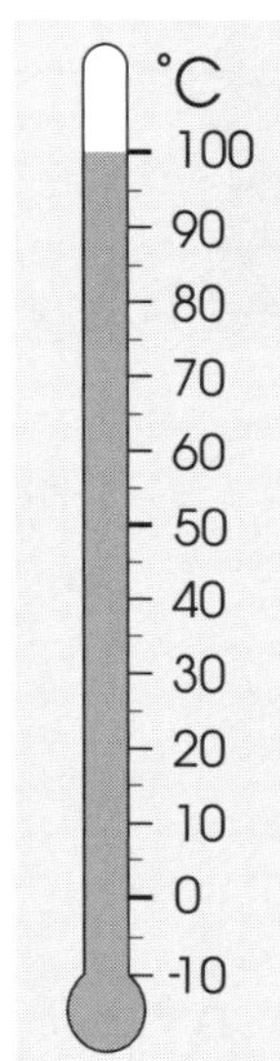

Good Business

Read what Mrs. Fare says. Write numbers on the grapes and fill in the blank.

There are 90 bags of grapes in my store. If 4 bags of grapes are sold each hour, how many bags of grapes will be left after 8 hours?

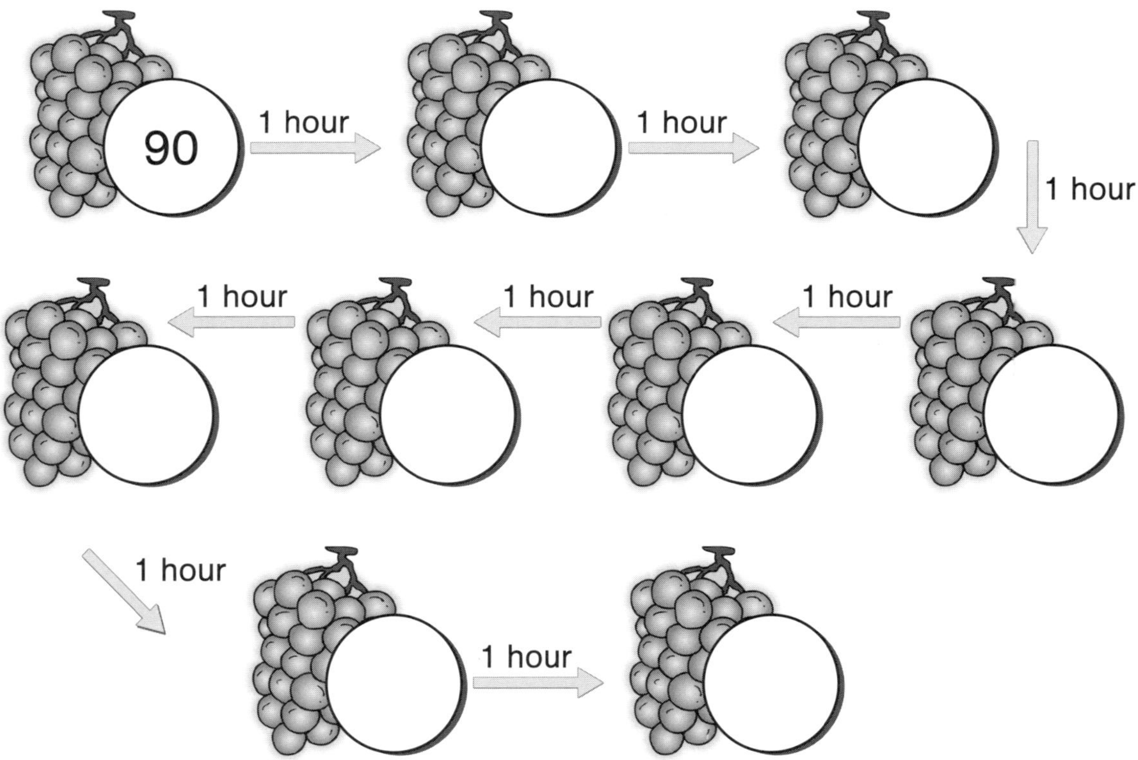

After 8 hours, _____ bags of grapes will be left.

44 Edith's Shapes

Edith has cut a lot of shapes. Look at them and answer Edith's questions.

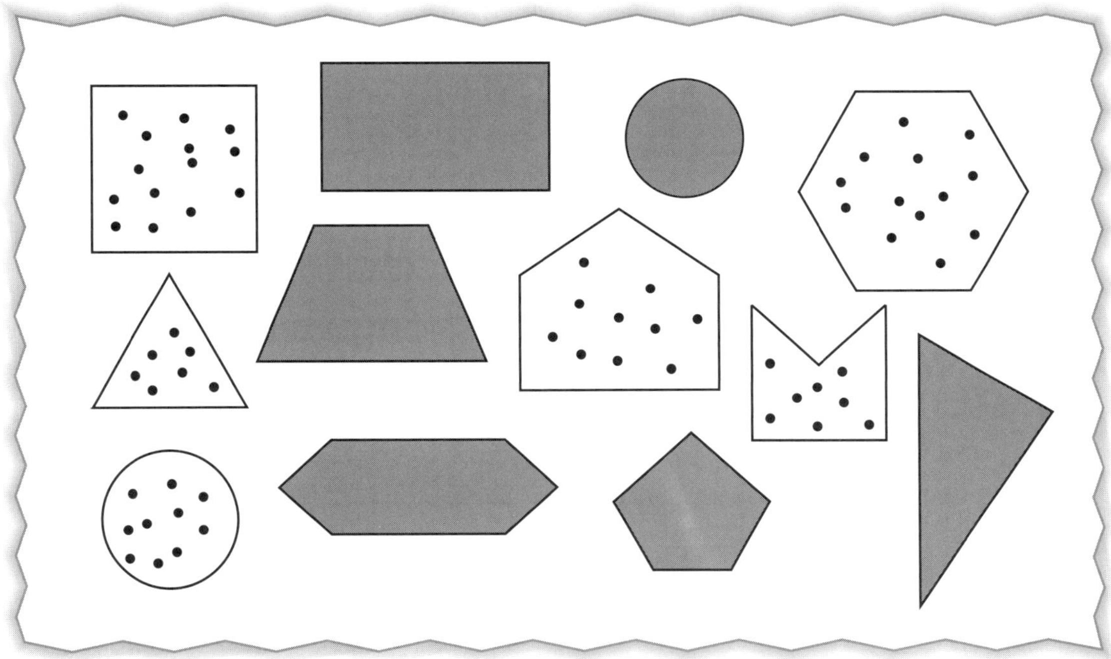

What fraction of the shapes

① have 4 sides? ________

② have 5 sides? ________

③ have 6 sides? ________

④ are triangles? ________

⑤ have dots? ________

45 Buying Drinks

Help the people solve the problems.

①

If I pay a loonie for a can of pop, how much change will I get?

________ ¢

②

I had a quarter. I bought a box of juice. How much do I have now?

________ ¢

③

I have 38¢. If I buy a cup of coffee for my mom, how much more do I need?

________ ¢

④

Dad wants to buy two cups of tea. How much does he need to pay?

________ ¢